Kiss From The Rose: Holiday Reminiscence

Kate Beebe

BookLeaf Publishing

India | USA | UK

Kiss From The Rose: Holiday Reminiscence
© 2024 Kate Beebe

Presentation by *BookLeaf Publishing*

Web: www.bookleafpub.com

E-mail: info@bookleafpub.com

ISBN: 9789358313383

First edition 2024

*I dedicate this book to my mom and dad,
who always encouraged me to try my best
in everything I did. Thank you.*

PREFACE

When I saw the chance to get my poetry published, I immediately took it. Right after, I thought to myself, "I have no idea what I'm going to write." As I write this preface I still don't exactly know what this collection of poetry will entail. It may just be terrible haikus about snow. However, I have a goal and a mission to write about my experiences at Christmastime and whether you'd like to experience it with me is entirely up to you. Basically, this book is a Christmas present to me so I hope it's good. And if you like it, then it's my Christmas gift to you. If you don't like it, there's always next year.

Home for the Holidays

Coming home feels so strange
When you've been away for so long
You already can't wait to go back
Even though you missed it all so much

They love being home for the holidays
But holidays can only go on for so long
It's important because it's one day of the year
Then why are they still here?

I created a home for myself
But it's so far away from my own
I want to get back to living life
It's nobody's fault but mine
I'm just having a difficult time
I need life to get back to normal
My life needs to once again be mine

Dear Christmas Tree

Oh Christmas tree,
You're so beautiful
God's gift to us this year
Oh Christmas tree
Who would've thought
We stole you away
Oh, dear

I promise Christmas tree
We didn't mean to take you
To steal you from a nice family
Or an sweet couple
who cut you down
It was an accident, Christmas tree
Please forgive us
'Tis the season for miracles

We're very sorry sweet Christmas tree
We didn't notice until it was too late
But you are this year's gift to us
And a story to tell

Love, Kate

From: Dad

The last gift I was given from him was socks
Red and white argyle that said 'cow' on the top
of the foot
He won them online and thought I'd like them
I wore them so much the holes in the soles were
endless
I stopped wearing them long ago
But I still keep them
with my passport
A special place
For the last gift he gave to me
For the last time he thought of me
And something I might like
For the first Christmas without him.
I think I got my first phone that year too
But I still have the socks
And I still ask for socks
Every year

Decorating

So many ornaments
So little time
How do we get them all up?
Let's simply go through each one
At least our favorites
Will be enough

The little pink panther
Made of pipe cleaners
thrills me every December
The crystal ornaments I made for mothers day
In the second grade
Still find a way to get on the tree
Little stocking and momentums from life get put
up
'Joy' spelled backwards is a treasured joke
Coming from our strange family
Christmas is about the little things
And ornaments are as small as it gets
But don't forget about the lights
We still put them up even though
they're a real bitch

Kiss From a Rose For Christmas

Christmas music comes up every December
Usually right after Thanksgiving
I've listened for years and I
Know all the words
But one song hits more than ever
Seal sang it best
It's his Greatest Hit
We sang it nonstop Christmas Day
The only thing that I can compare it to
Is a kiss from a rose on the grey

My Snow Haiku

6

Freshly fallen snow
Crunching sounds beneath the ground
Makes me want cocoa

Christmas Baking

The shaking of the brown paper bag
Sadly a workout, still
a rush of adrenaline passes through
with each rattle
It sounds like a winter storm.
The smell of powdered sugar
appearing as fresh snow
cold yet delicious.
The sweetness of chocolate
Melted, silky smooth
Signifying the richness of Christmas
The joy of a memory
Is way better than the taste
Still delicious

The Advent

Four candles to burn
Each take a turn
To help us remember ourselves.
No matter your beliefs
Must recognize the distinct
Importance of four simple nouns

Hope.
A glimmering piece of wonder
Caught and kept through broken eyes
Peace.
Stillness and quiet
In turbulent times
Joy.
The laughter and smiles
Of those we keep near
Love.
The ultimate feeling
That shows how deeply we care.

God Our King in This Economy?

Politics are kinda shit
But I guess religion is too
Atheists are fucking stupid
But pastors can be absolutely cruel

If you follow His word
How come you all have different beliefs?
If I have to interpret it myself
Then I guess His word comes from Me

I'm too old to stop believing
And I'm too young to go to hell
But I truly don't understand
Why I can't just be myself

And when I die
And become truly holy
Just like the big man upstairs,
I'll be entirely boring.

(But at least there won't be politicians)

Every Night I Lie Awake

Every night I lie awake
And dream of love
A type of love to cause rebellion
Breaking every rule for that single individual
And when I lie there
Thinking about who they are
Their perfections and flaws
I realize they are no one
Because I can never have a lawless love
If there is no law to be broken

Cheeeeese

I'm just a little piece of cheese
With no cracker of salami
Don't leave me out or else I'll stink
Cause I am here for you to eat
I'll be honest that's my kink
Yeah, I might be into vore
I guess I'm just a cheesy whore

Where Lost Things Go

I act like a kid
And I sound like one too
But my thoughts are on constant loop.
My bustling mind
Holds a theory of mine
That might quite ever delight you.
While people whisk away
to Heaven or Hell
Their lost things deserve the World
It's unfair that while we get to go Somewhere
Else
They must stay completely still

It's a wild hypothesis
but ever the optimist
I hope to be right in every way
Since I lost my best stuffy
When I was six years old
and I still think about Him
to this day.

Now I could be wrong
But my heart still belongs
To a little moose with a red scarf
So I pray lost things go to a place to be loved
While we continue to grow
and fall apart

Conviction

The boy has no conviction
He's as supercilious as a worm
Nothing new can phase him
Is he smart or a cowardice germ?
The boy lacks such conviction
showing others he's convinced
Is a task so difficult for this little boy
You would think his entirety is indifference
The boy is too comfortable for conviction
too scared to lose what he has
His beliefs and opinions
Mean nothing to him
The boy's life is so
Incredibly sad
The boy needs his conviction
To stop worrying about what we think
Though we may not agree
Doesn't mean we will leave
The boy is such a sweet fink

Little Sailboat

Rusty little sailboat
Are you okay?
You're all torn and beaten up
But you still manage to stay afloat

Rugged little sailboat
Though you're all stripped away,
Your bright blue paint
Shines through your scars
It's as clear as day

Broken little sailboat
No choices can you make
The ocean tides carry and you
must comply with them all-day

No options for you little sailboat
You blow with the wind and
ride out the storms
It's very brave but to you
just another day

Don't worry little sailboat
I'll fix you up as best I can
Cover the scars, put you on the bay

So you can finally decide
your coordinates today.

15

Now I Have a Machine Gun

I watched Diehard five times this December
And it only gets better and better
I could recite the whole thing
Yet I still enjoying watching
it brings me so much joy
Even though I know what happens
I root for Roy.
He takes out all the terrorists
One by one by one
He blows up the entire building
And inevitably drops Hans
Gerrero becomes McClaine
As John saves the day
He came out to the coast for only a few laughs
But he's still yelling
Yippee ki-yay

Never Enough Time

My grandfather loved rhubarb pie
we'd bake pies, my grandma
And I loved to spend time with her
Spending the night in her spare room
When I never had one to myself,
It felt like a hotel
But we'd bake and craft
She'd let me paint and sometimes
I'd eat from the sugar bowl
Like fun dip
She gave me so many memories
And maybe diabetes
but it was so worth it to
Have a grandma who loved me like her
for a while

Thirst

So dry
Sahara desert in the hot daytime
it's so dark outside
I can't tell the time
I wish I wish I wish
But dreams can only last so long
waking is the hard part
you feel most alive but
still want to die
And go back before you felt that
Dry feeling inside
It bubbles up and eats your entire
self, still
you try to survive
Reach for what you're made of
and understand
life.
Cool and tasteless
Yet so delicious
Not too basic or acidic
Drink it up,
the nectar of life
Is so close
You just have to take it.

Gifts I've Lost

One was afraid of storms but was the best
One was a mess who still cared for us
One was old fashioned but so curious
One I barely knew but worked till he died
One cared for her family all her life
One was a stoic man who always did his part
And lastly is the one I loved with all my heart

Two got old and we never saw
One I put down and had to stay strong
One I avoided because I couldn't face death
One I was there for her
And one I left
The last one happened all too fast

Gone too soon and still in mind
I think about them every day,
All the time
Especially during the Christmas season
Who I am today
They're the reason